THE *Caroler's* HANDBOOK

Contemporary Settings of Holiday Favorites For Concert, Show, or Caroling

SATB

Arranged by MARK HANSON
Compiled and edited by TEENA CHINN

TABLE OF CONTENTS

Cover Design : Robert Ramsay

INTRODUCTION TO CAROL SINGING

THE CAROLER'S HANDBOOK provides a fresh, new approach to the standard carols we have come to associate with the holiday season. Although each *a cappella* choral setting has been designed to enhance the inherent characteristics of the original carol, no two carols have been approached in exactly the same way. This adds a vitality and versatility to the HANDBOOK seldom found in collections of this type, while, in the meantime, providing the choral director with a dynamic and versatile tool for use in his or her holiday program planning. The following is a list of considerations and performance suggestions you may want to keep in mind when using the HANDBOOK.

WHO SHOULD USE THIS BOOK: Groups of all sizes, at all musical levels and of all ages will enjoy the new treatment of these seasonal favorites. Although written with the average high school choir in mind, the handbook can and should be used by Concert Choirs, Show/Jazz Choirs, Church Choirs, Community Choruses as well as individual SATB quartets. A keyboard may provide basic support.

WHERE TO USE THIS BOOK: In addition to standard holiday concertizing, THE CAROLER'S HANDBOOK is appropriate for use in virtually every caroling situation. Consider taking it with you to shopping malls, hospitals, airports, convalescent homes, condos, private Christmas parties, as well as the halls at school.

STANDING FORMATION: Since these carols are designed to be performed *a cappella,* careful consideration should be taken in the placement of the various vocal parts, The smaller ensemble will most likely achieve best results by standing in a semi-circle. Individuals may be placed together in sections,

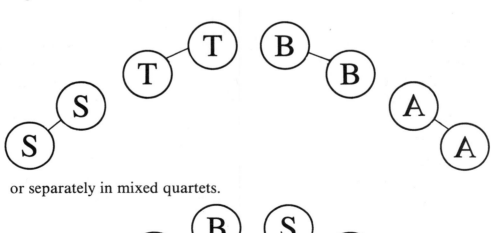

or separately in mixed quartets.

For the larger ensemble, the following formation is suggested:

BASS	TENOR
SOPRANO	ALTO

This placement serves three purposes. It

    1) places the males and females next to each other from left to right, thus facilitating blend.

    2) positions the outer and inner voices next to each other from front to back, thus assisting intonation (especially in the outer voices),

and

    3) places each part nearest to the section closest to it from high to low, thus enabling each voice to hear the part on either side of it in the part-writing.

VOCAL PRODUCTION: Proper breath support and tonal focus are essential for successful performance of these carols. A clear and crisp enunciation of consonants should occur in the up tempo songs, while a softer treatment is suggested for the slower pieces. An effective performance can be achieved by striving for a warm tone with a small amount of vibrato.

Treatment of each piece should dictate its interpretation. Allow for linear phrases, gentle nuances and rubatos to occur in the ballad selections, while keeping the swing style songs in tempo with a light staccato articulation.

PROGRAMMING ALTERNATIVES: Once you begin working with THE CAROLER'S HANDBOOK, you will see that the ways of utilizing it are virtually endless.

The chart below lists each title, its style of arrangement, key, meter and tempo.

SONG TITLE	STYLE	KEY	METER	TEMPO
Angels We Have Heard On High	Quasi-spiritual	G	$\frac{4}{4}$	Moderate
Away In A Manger	Homophonic	G	$\frac{3}{4}$	Slow
Chanukah, O Chanukah	Patter	F	$\frac{4}{4}$	Mod. Fast
The First Noel	Homophonic	C	$\frac{3}{4}$	Slow
Hark! The Herald Angels Sing	Homophonic	G	$\frac{4}{4}$	Mod. Slow
Have Yourself A Merry Little Christmas	Mild Jazz	C	$\frac{4}{4}$	Slow
A Holly Jolly Christmas	Hint of Swing	C	$\frac{4}{4}$	Moderate
I'll Be Home For Christmas	Mild Jazz	C	$\frac{4}{4}$	Mod. Slow
Jingle Bells	Gentle Swing	G	$\frac{4}{4}$	Moderate
Joy To The World	Sprightly 6/8	C	$\frac{6}{8}$	Moderate
Let It Snow! Let It Snow! Let It Snow!	Softshoe Swing	F	$\frac{4}{4}$	Moderate
Merry Christmas, Darling	Mild Jazz	D	$\frac{4}{4}$	Slow
O Christmas Tree	Homophonic	F	$\frac{3}{4}$	Slow
O Come, All Ye Faithful	Homophonic	G	$\frac{4}{4}$	Mod. Slow
Rudolph, The Red-Nosed Reindeer	Trad. with Alt. Bass	C	$\frac{4}{4}$	Mod. Fast
Santa Claus Is Comin' To Town	Swing Jazzy	C	$\frac{4}{4}$	Moderate
Silent Night	Homophonic	C	$\frac{3}{4}$	Slow
Silver Bells	Waltz	Bb	$\frac{3}{4}$	Moderate

Here are several possibilities.

1. Sing two or three carols from the handbook as a vignette at your holiday program. By combining songs of complimentary theme, style and/or key relationship a number of "mini-medleys" can be created. For example, three secular carols arranged in swing style work great together to form:

A SWINGIN' CHRISTMAS!
(A medley of carols including:)
JINGLE BELLS
LET IT SNOW! LET IT SNOW! LET IT SNOW!
A HOLLY JOLLY CHRISTMAS

Or, for something different, put three calmer, sacred carols in a vignette entitled:

OUR GENTLE SAVIOR
(A medley of homage to the Christ Child, including:)
AWAY IN A MANGER
HARK! THE HERALD ANGELS SING
THE FIRST NOEL

2. For even greater variety, begin with a "standard" version of a carol; then, part-way through, switch to the HANDBOOK's version/harmonization. For example, you might begin with a stately rendition of "Angels We Have Heard On High" before directly segueing to the HANDBOOK's spiritual version. Other HANDBOOK arrangements lending themselves especially well to this are:

AWAY IN A MANGER
HARK! THE HERALD ANGELS SING
JINGLE BELLS
JOY TO THE WORLD
O COME, ALL YE FAITHFUL
SILENT NIGHT

STAGING: Changing the "picture" on the stage not only adds interest and variety to a program, but also assists in bringing the performance to the desired relaxation and climax points. One relatively simple staging method is to group your ensemble on platforms of various heights. Alter the visual image shape of the ensemble by moving select members at appropriate intervals, such as the end of a musical vignette. Have several members of the ensemble seated (with straight backs!) on the taller platforms during the quieter selections. Move the ensemble into a straight line on the lip of the stage to perform a novelty piece (adding line-type choreography) and then out into the audience for the final selection.

CHORALOGRAPHY: The implementation of appropriate choralography will bring beautiful visual and aural results to your performance. This can be achieved by combining sign language with simple dramatic gestures. My rule of thumb is to keep the movement simple, thereby allowing it to be graceful and stunning. Care should be taken to allow the movement to appear smooth and natural.

Slight variances throughout the selection provide for greater impact with minimal rehearsal time. For example, begin SILENT NIGHT with a single member of the chorus in interpretive motion, then add members one at a time as the song progresses so that the entire ensemble moves in reverence to the text, "Jesus, Lord at Thy birth."

USE OF STAGING/CHORALOGRAPHY: Any staging or movement should always function to enhance the music. If the group configuration or choralography you've designed upstages the musical elements of the song, remove it. Let the music speak for itself *first,* then add the dimensions of staging and movement.

May THE CAROLER'S HANDBOOK bring added satisfaction and joy to your celebration of the Holiday season!

Mark Hanson

6

SILVER BELLS

Begin this carol slowly, with reminiscence and melancholy. Then, bounce into the waltz
feel (in one) at measure 18. Try to resist the urge to slow down at measure 34, being
sure to maintain a sense of buoyancy. M.H.

Words and Music by
JAY LIVINGSTON and RAY EVANS
Arranged by MARK HANSON

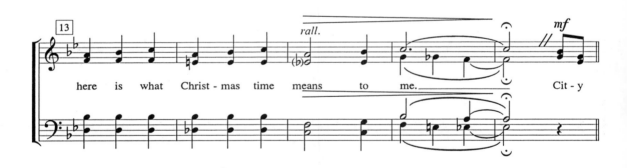

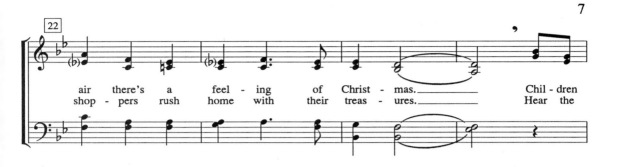

air there's a feel - ing of Christ - mas. _____ Chil - dren
shop - pers rush home with their treas - ures. _____ Hear the

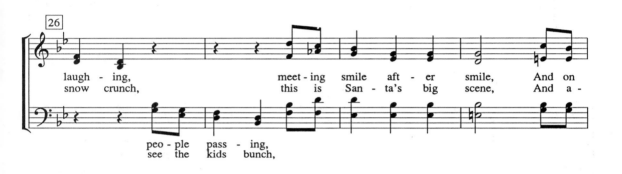

laugh - ing, meet - ing smile aft - er smile, And on
snow crunch, this is San - ta's big scene, And a -

peo - ple pass - ing,
see the kids bunch,

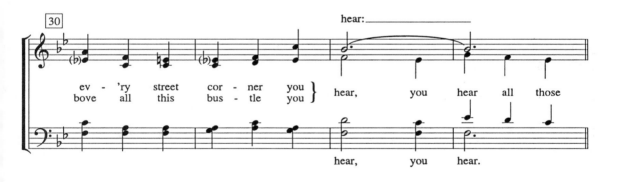

hear: _____

ev - 'ry street cor - ner you } hear, you hear all those
bove all this bus - tle you

hear, you hear.

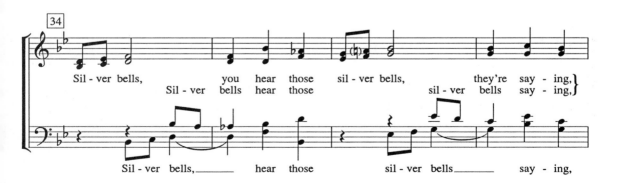

Sil - ver bells, you hear those sil - ver bells, they're say - ing, }
Sil - ver bells hear those sil - ver bells say - ing, }

Sil - ver bells, _____ hear those sil - ver bells _____ say - ing,

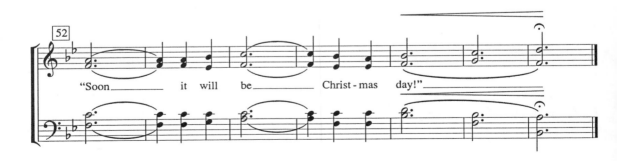

JOY TO THE WORLD

Be sure to differentiate between the 4/4 and 6/8 feel in measures 13-16. The male voices should sound like church bells tolling the news of the Christmas season. Try raising the key up 1/2-step (to D-flat) in measure 26 before singing the third verse. M.H.

Words by ISAAC WATTS
Music by GEORGE F. HANDEL
Arranged by MARK HANSON

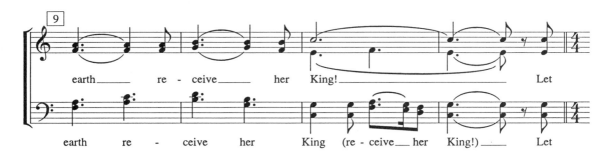

10

Additional verses:

2. Joy to the world! The Saviour reigns;
   Let men their songs employ,
   While fields and floods
   Rocks, hills, and plains,
   Repeat the sounding joy,
   Repeat the sounding joy,
   Repeat, repeat the sounding joy.

3. He rules the world with truth and grace,
   And makes the nations prove
   The glories of
   His righteousness,
   And wonders of His love,
   And wonders of His love,
   And wonders, wonders of His love.

LET IT SNOW! LET IT SNOW! LET IT SNOW!

Your basses and tenors will love singing this one! Lean into the chromatic passages (ms, 18, 20, and 22), enjoying the interplay as it occurs between the male and female voices. Accent each successive entrance at the beginning and take off! M. H.

Lyric by SAMMY CAHN
Music by JULE STYNE
Arranged by MARK HANSON

SILENT NIGHT

This soothing text with its subtle vocal shadings should be approached as a prayer. Feel free to be very liberal with the tempo. A soloist singing the words with the remaining ensemble humming always works well with this carol. M.H.

Lyric by JOSEPH MOHR
Music by FRANZ GRUBER
Arranged by MARK HANSON

EL03636

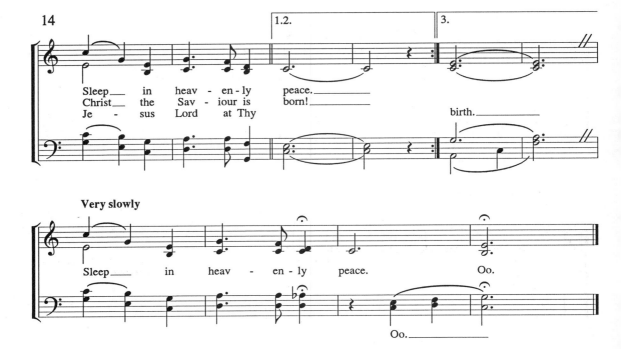

Sleep___ in heav - en-ly peace.___
Christ___ the Sav - iour is born!___
Je - sus Lord at Thy birth.___

Very slowly

Sleep___ in heav - en-ly peace. Oo.

Oo.___

RUDOLPH, THE RED-NOSED REINDEER

You might want to add a bit of movement to this one. Start with a gentle sway from left to right at measure 8. Have the guys lean in on the "echoing" parts (e.g.: "had a shiny one" and "he said."). The entire ensemble can strike a pose as they shake jazz hands in measure 38 to give it a flashy finish! M.H.

Words and Music by
JOHNNY MARKS
Arranged by MARK HANSON

mf

SA

You know Dash - er and Danc - er and Pranc - er and Vix - en,

mf

TB

Com - et and Cu - pid and Don - ner and Blitz - en, but do you re -

ANGELS WE HAVE HEARD ON HIGH

You can't stand still to sing this one! Try moving the key up 1/2 step (to an A-flat chord) in measure 27 before going on to the additional verse. You might want to use this piece as a processional to begin your program. M.H.

TRADITIONAL
Arranged by MARK HANSON

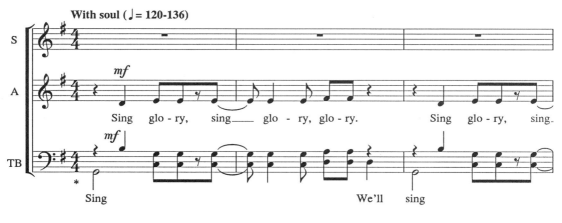

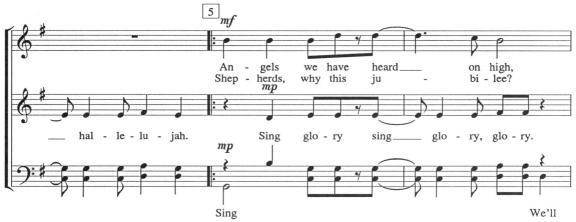

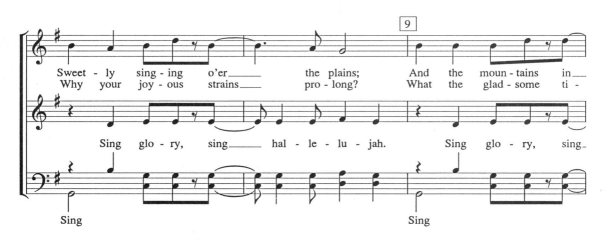

* If the range of the first line "g" is problematic, sing it up an octave throughout piece.

EL03636

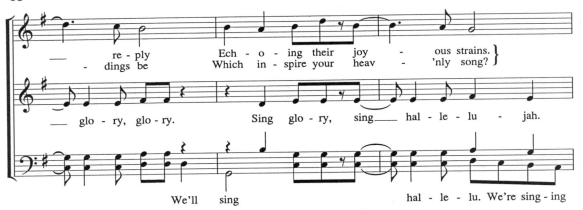

re - ply / - dings be
Ech - o - ing their joy - ous strains. } / Which in - spire your heav - 'nly song? }

glo - ry, glo - ry. Sing glo - ry, sing___ hal - le - lu - jah.

We'll sing hal - le - lu. We're sing - ing

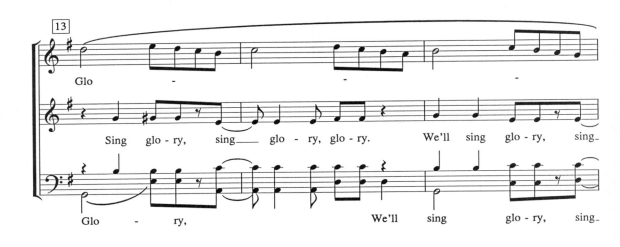

Glo - - -

Sing glo - ry, sing___ glo - ry, glo - ry. We'll sing glo - ry, sing___

Glo - ry, We'll sing glo - ry, sing___

- ri - a in ex - cel - sis De - o,

___ hal - le - lu in ex - cel - sis De - o.___

___ glo - ri - a. We're sing - ing in ex - cel - sis De - o. We'll

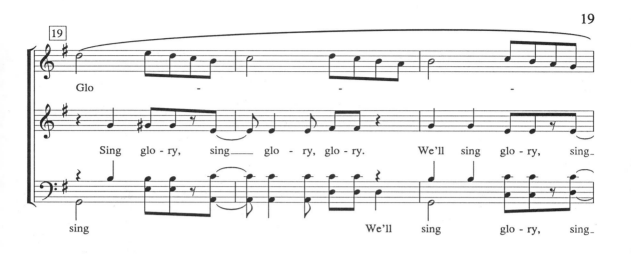

Glo - - -

Sing glo-ry, sing___ glo-ry, glo-ry. We'll sing glo-ry, sing___

sing   We'll   sing   glo-ry,   sing___

- ri - a   in ex-cel-sis De - o.___

___ hal-le-lu   in ex-cel-sis De - o. Sing glo-ry, sing___

___ glo-ri-a. We're sing-ing in ex-cel-sis De - o. We'll sing

___ glo-ry, glo-ry.   Sing glo-ry, sing___ hal-le-lu-jah.

We'll   sing

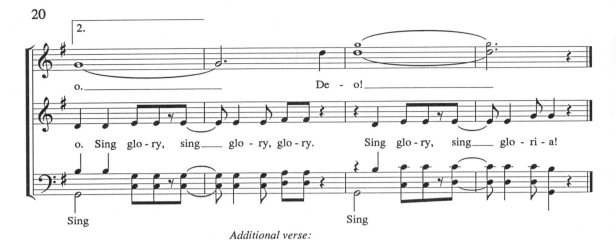

Additional verse:

Come to Bethlehem and see
Him whose birth the angels sing;
Come adore on bended knee
Christ the Lord, the newborn King.
Refrain

SANTA CLAUS IS COMIN' TO TOWN

This straightforward arrangement works great as a singalong. Encourage the ensemble to "bounce" the text, especially on the echo parts (ms. 8-9, 11-12, 27-28 and 30). This is another song that lends itself well to staging/choreography applications. M.H.

Words by HAVEN GILLESPIE
Music by J. FRED COOTS
Arranged by MARK HANSON

O COME, ALL YE FAITHFUL

Try not to let the tempo of this piece get too fast, thus losing the feeling of reverence that
is indicated. You may want to point out the other Christmas carol that is implied at the
beginning of this work. M.H.

Words translated by
FREDERICK OAKLEY and others
Music from
JOHN F. WADE'S CANTUS DIVERSI
Arranged by MARK HANSON

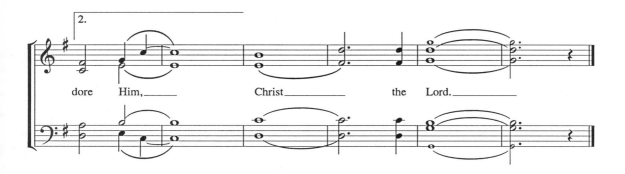

HAVE YOURSELF A
MERRY LITTLE CHRISTMAS

Don't shy away from this arrangement because it may look hard! Extra care was taken to keep the voice leadings smooth and logical and the rhythmic motives constant. Work to produce a straight tone with pure vowel sounds throughout the chart, taking lots of liberties with the tempo. M.H.

Words and Music by
HUGH MARTIN and RALPH BLANE
Arranged by MARK HANSON

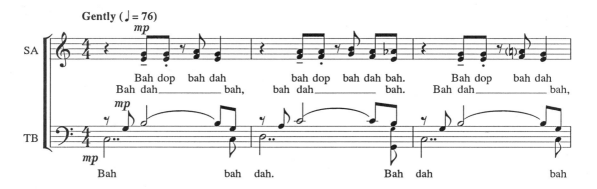

24

HARK! THE HERALD ANGELS SING

This arrangement was conceived to emanate the sense of awe and wonder that surely was present at the birth of the Christ Child. Beginning almost as a lullaby, each verse should become more joyous as the angels "leave" the quiet surroundings of the manger to fill the heavens with the glorious message of His birth. M.H.

Lyric by CHARLES WESLEY
Music by FELIX MENDELSSOHN
Arranged by MARK HANSON

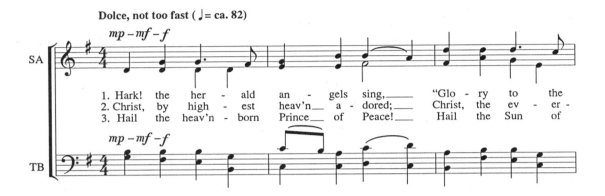

1. Hark! the her - ald an - gels sing,___ "Glo - ry to the
2. Christ, by high - est heav'n a - dored;___ Christ, the ev - er -
3. Hail the heav'n - born Prince of Peace!___ Hail the Sun of

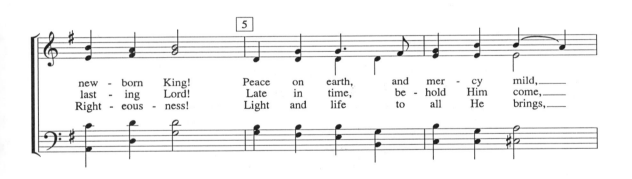

new - born King! Peace on earth, and mer - cy mild,___
last - ing Lord! Late in time, be - hold Him come,___
Right - eous - ness! Light and life to all He brings,___

God and sin - ners re - con - ciled." Joy - ful all ye
Off - spring of a vir - gin's womb. Veiled in flesh the
Ris'n with heal - ing in His wings. Mild, He lays His

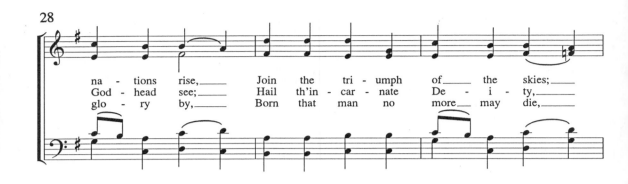

na - tions rise,___ Join the tri - umph of___ the skies;___
God - head see;___ Hail th'in - car - nate De - i - ty,___
glo - ry by,___ Born that man no more___ may die,___

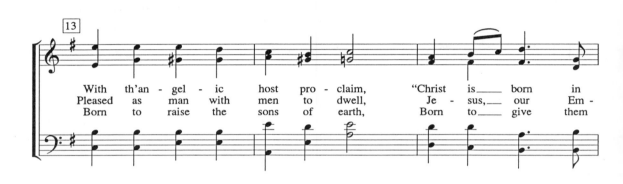

With th'an - gel - ic host pro - claim, "Christ is___ born in
Pleased as man with men to dwell, Je - sus,___ our Em -
Born to raise the sons of earth, Born to___ give them

Beth - le - hem."___ Hark! the her - ald an - gels sing,___ "Glo - ry to the
man - u - el.___ Hark! the her - ald an - gels sing,___ "Glo - ry___ to the
sec - ond birth.___ Hark! the her - ald an - gels sing,___ "Glo - ry___ to the

1.2.
new - born King!"
new - born King!"

3.
new - born King!" The new - born King!

f *rit.*

MERRY CHRISTMAS, DARLING

Use a little more motion to assist in contrasting measures 25-28 from the rest of the song. Take time, especially at the ends of phrases, allowing for much expression. The use of one or more soloists may prove very effective for this setting. M.H.

Lyric by
FRANK POOLER
Music by
RICHARD CARPENTER
Arranged by
MARK HANSON

A HOLLY JOLLY CHRISTMAS

Be sure to point out the interplay between voices occuring throughout this arrangement. You may want to slow down the last two measures of the second ending and let the basses ham it up a little! Add finger snaps on beats two and four to help the swing feel, if you like. M.H.

Words and Music by
JOHNNY MARKS
Arranged by
MARK HANSON

down the street___ Say hel - lo to friends you know and

Hel - lo friends know

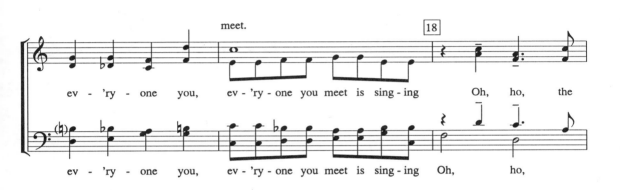

meet.

ev - 'ry - one you, ev - 'ry - one you meet is sing - ing Oh, ho, the

ev - 'ry - one you, ev - 'ry - one you meet is sing - ing Oh, ho,

toe___ see.

mis - tle - toe___ is hung where you can see it hang - ing.

mis - tle - toe___ is hung where you can see.

Some - bod - y waits for you,___ kiss her once for me.___

Some - one waits for you,___ you're gon - na kiss her once for, kiss___

Have a hol - ly jol - ly Christ - mas and in
_ her once for me and have a Hol - ly jol - ly

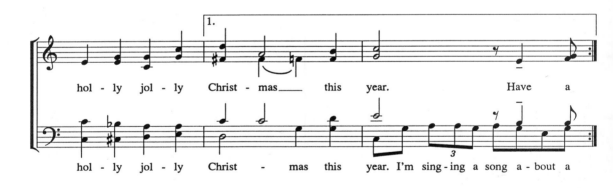

hear___ cresc.
case you did-n't hear___ the song I'm sing-ing to you. Oh, by gol-ly, have a
cresc.
case you did-n't hear___ I'm say-ing Oh, by gol-ly, have a

1.
hol - ly jol - ly Christ - mas___ this year. Have a
hol - ly jol - ly Christ - mas this year. I'm sing-ing a song a - bout a

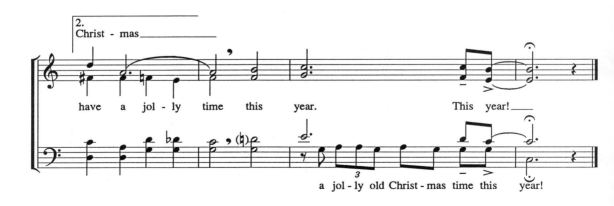

2.
Christ - mas___
have a jol - ly time this year. This year!___
a jol - ly old Christ - mas time this year!

AWAY IN A MANGER

This little lullaby is one of my personal favorites. Feel free to let the tempo drift with the tension and relaxation of the harmonies. Caress the text, singing as gently and sweetly as you can. For more variety, designate a soloist singing the melody of a given section (vs. 2, ms. 1-16, for example) while the remaining ensemble "oo's." M.H.

Lyric by
MARTIN LUTHER
Music by
JONATHAN E. SPILLMAN
Arranged by
MARK HANSON

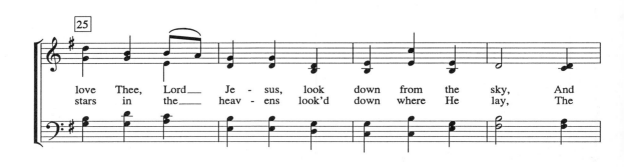

O CHRISTMAS TREE

This straightforward setting adds subtle shadings to an all-time Christmas classic. Keep the tempo slow, the mood reminiscent. M.H.

OLD GERMAN CAROL
Arranged by
MARK HANSON

Christ - mas Tree,_____ You share a won - d'rous mess - age.

Additional verses:

O Christmas Tree, O Christmas Tree,
O tree of green, unchanging.
O Christmas Tree, O Christmas Tree,
O tree of green, unchanging.
Your boughs, so green in summertime,
Do brave the snow of wintertime.
O Christmas Tree, O Christmas Tree,
O Tree of green, unchanging.

O Christmas Tree, O Christmas Tree,
You set my heart a-singing.
O Christmas Tree, O Christmas Tree,
You set my heart a-singing.
Like little stars, your candles bright
Send to the world a wondrous light.
O Christmas Tree, O Christmas Tree,
You set my heart a-singing.

I'LL BE HOME FOR CHRISTMAS

This setting suggests a somewhat breathy sound, while maintaining full support in keeping a smooth legato feel throughout. Try to sing 8 measures on a breath at bars 9 and 17, allowing each phrase to arch and swell in accordance with the text. M.H.

Words and Music by
KIM GANNON, WALTER KENT
and BUCK RAM
Arranged by
MARK HANSON

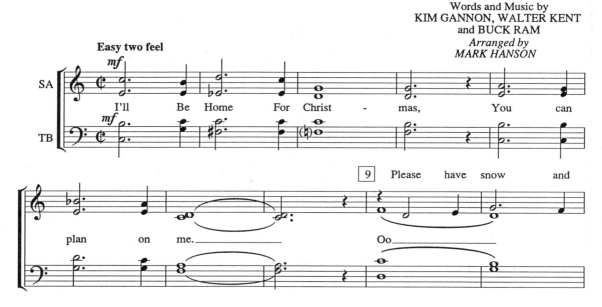

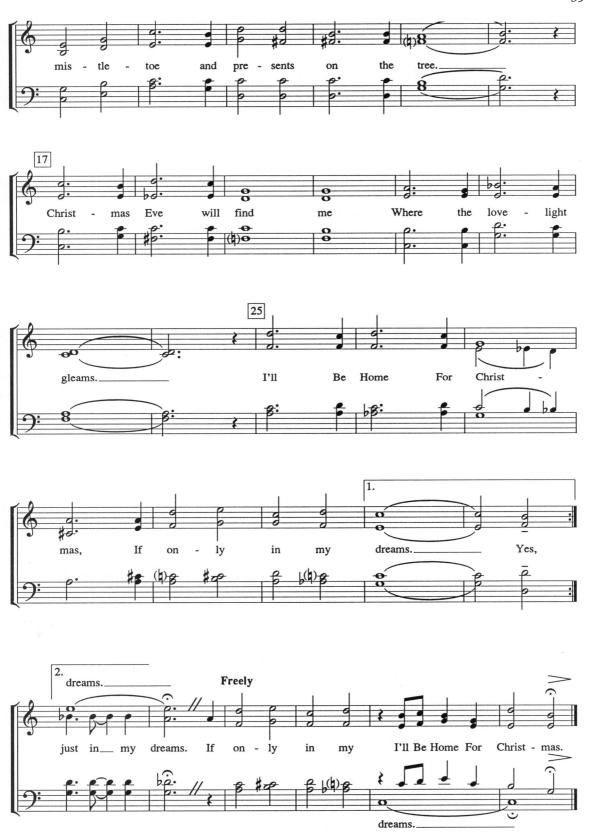

THE FIRST NOEL

The word "simplice" comes to mind when considering this setting; keep it simple. You might want to alternate verses between full ensemble and solo with choir "oo" back-up. For an optional ending, sing measures 17-22 (with the pick-up) an additional time before proceeding to the final ending. M.H.

TRADITIONAL
Arranged by
MARK HANSON

deep. No - el,_____ No - el, No - el, No -

el,_____ Born is the King_____ of Is - ra -

el. Is - ra - el.

2. They looked up and saw a star
   Shining in the East, beyond them far;
   And to the earth it gave great light,
   And so it continued both day and night.

   Refrain

3. And by the light of that same star,
   Three wise men came from country far;
   To seek for a King was their intent,
   And to follow the star wherever it went.

   Refrain

4. This star drew nigh to the northwest,
   O'er Bethlehem it took its rest;
   And there it did both stop and stay,
   Right over the place where Jesus lay.

   Refrain

5. Then entered in those wise men three,
   Full reverently upon their knee;
   And offered there in His presence,
   Their gold, and myrrh, and frankincense.

   Refrain

JINGLE BELLS

You've heard of *rocking* around the Christmas tree? Well, this is *Swingin'* those jingle bells! The basses will love their boogie woogie "string-bass" line, while the altos and tenors sing teasingly on the afterbeat. Just don't have too much fun that you cover up the melody! M.H.

J. PIERPONT
Arranged by
MARK HANSON

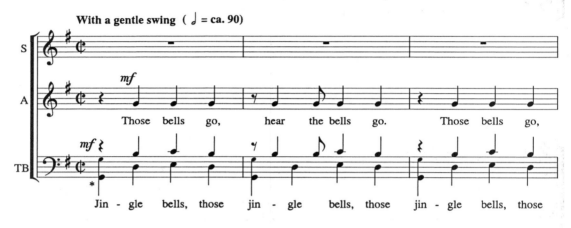

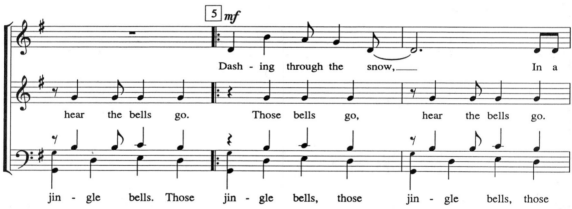

* Sing cued notes if range is a problem.

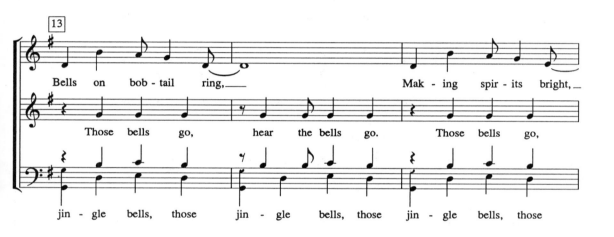

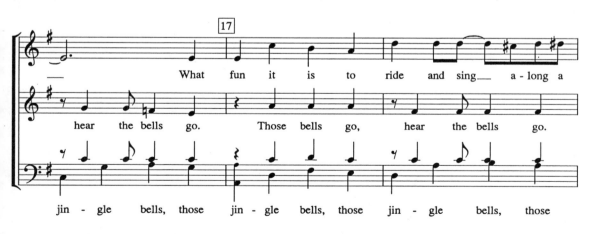

EL03636

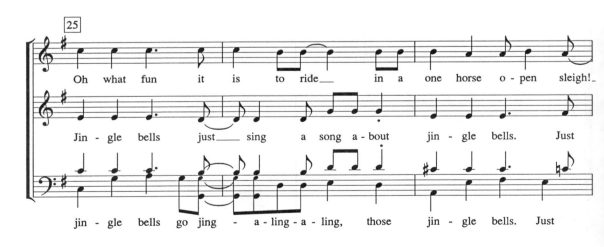

EL03636

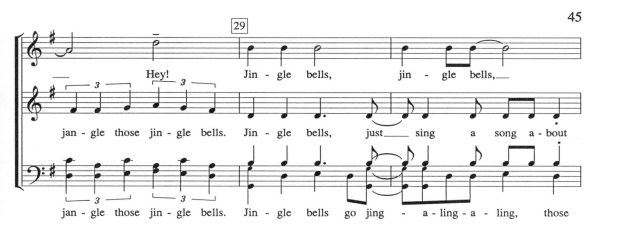

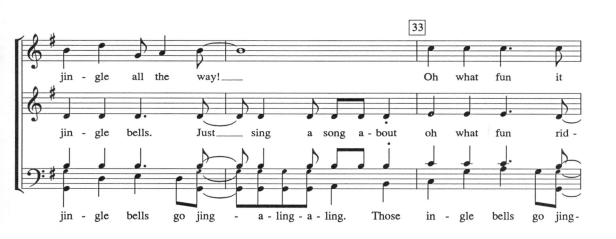

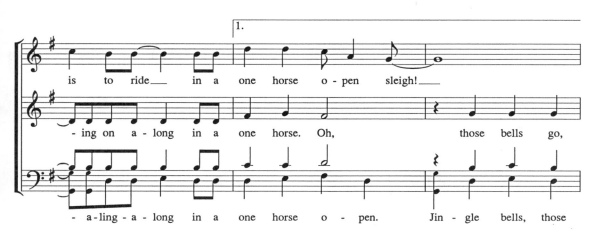

* May be shouted, "whinnied" or "neighed".

2. A day or two ago,
   Well, I thought I'd take a ride;
   Soon Miss Fanny Bright sat right by my side.
   Horse was lean and lank,
   Fortune seemed his lot;
   He got into a drifted bank
   And then a-we, we got upsot!

3. Now the ground is white,
   So just go it while you're young.
   Take the girls tonight; sing this sleighing song.
   Get a bobtail nag, two-forty his speed
   And hitch him to an open sleigh
   And with a crack you'll take the lead!

For Christine, Denise and Stephanie

CHANUKAH, O CHANUKAH

Make sure that the bass and tenor ostinato doesn't overpower the alto and soprano lines. Alternate from a staccato articulation in measures 3-10 to a more legato interpretation in measures 11-18. You might want to add finger cymbals or tambourine throughout (♩♫♩♫) with a 2-measure introduction. For even more variety, sing the song as a two-part arrangement for female voices! M.H.

Arranged by
MARK HANSON

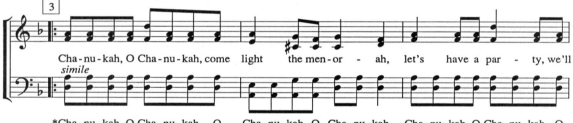

* Don't cover melody

EL03636

48

(Top system, m. 8) *cresc. poco a poco*

play - ing, the can - dles are burn - ing low;

cresc. poco a poco

play - ing, can - dles, the can - dles are burn - ing, they're burn - ing, they're

(m. 15)

one for each night, they shed a sweet light to re - mind us of days long a -

one for each night, they shed a sweet light, re - mind us of days long. O

(m. 20)

1. *f* go.

O go.

2. *f* go. One for each night they

Cha - nu - kah, O Cha - nu - kah. Cha - nu - kah, O Cha - nu - kah. One for each night they

cresc. to end

shed a sweet light to re - mind us of

cresc. to end

shed a sweet light re - mind us, re - mind us, of

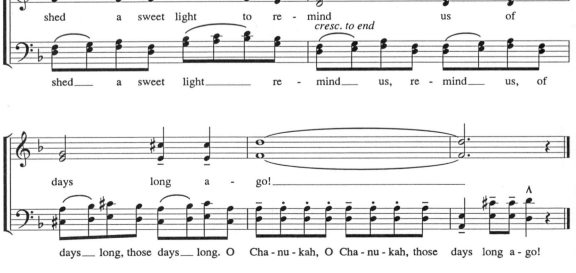

days long a - go!

days long, those days long. O Cha - nu - kah, O Cha - nu - kah, those days long a - go!

EL03636